369

Manifesting Workbook

This book belongs to:

_____

_____

_____

3 6 9 method MANIFESTIATION

🖊️ **WHAT?** The 369 method is writing manifesting technique that can be done to bring something or someone into your life by asking the universe.

🖊️ **HOW?** Every <u>Morning</u> write down what you want 3 times. Write it again around <u>midday</u>, 6 times. Lastly, write it again 9 times before you go to <u>bed</u>.

🖊️ **DO:** write "I will", "I have", "I do" <u>**BE PATIENT**</u>.

🖊️ **REMEMBER:** Think that you already have what you are asking the universe for.

🖊️ **THANK** the universe put all your faith and hands into the universe.

🖊️ **DON'T:** write "I want"

3 6 9

You can do it!

MANIFEST
3-6-9 contact method

1

2

3

1

2

3

4

5

6

1

2

3

4

5

6

7

8

9

MANIFEST
3-6-9 contact method

1

2

3

1

2

3

4

5

6

1

2

3

4

5

6

7

8

9

MANIFEST
3-6-9 contact method

1

2

3

1

2

3

4

5

6

1

2

3

4

5

6

7

8

9

MANIFEST
3-6-9 contact method

1

2

3

1

2

3

4

5

6

1

2

3

4

5

6

7

8

9

MANIFEST

3-6-9 contact method

1

2

3

1

2

3

4

5

6

1

2

3

4

5

6

7

8

9

MANIFEST
3-6-9 contact method

1

2

3

1

2

3

4

5

6

1

2

3

4

5

6

7

8

9

MANIFEST

3-6-9 contact method

1

2

3

1

2

3

4

5

6

1

2

3

4

5

6

7

8

9

MANIFEST
3-6-9 contact method

1

2

3

1

2

3

4

5

6

1

2

3

4

5

6

7

8

9

MANIFEST
3-6-9 contact method

Claim it!
TODAY'S DATE IS
_____

1

2

3

1

2

3

4

5

6

1

2

3

4

5

6

7

8

9

MANIFEST
3-6-9 contact method

1

2

3

1

2

3

4

5

6

1

2

3

4

5

6

7

8

9

MANIFEST
3-6-9 contact method

1

2

3

1

2

3

4

5

6

1

2

3

4

5

6

7

8

9

MANIFEST
3-6-9 contact method

1

2

3

1

2

3

4

5

6

1

2

3

4

5

6

7

8

9

MANIFEST
3-6-9 contact method

1

2

3

1

2

3

4

5

6

1

2

3

4

5

6

7

8

9

Claim it!
TODAY'S DATE IS
_____

MANIFEST
3-6-9 contact method

1

2

3

1

2

3

4

5

6

1

2

3

4

5

6

7

8

9

MANIFEST
3-6-9 contact method

1

2

3

1

2

3

4

5

6

1

2

3

4

5

6

7

8

9

MANIFEST
3-6-9 contact method

1

2

3

1

2

3

4

5

6

1

2

3

4

5

6

7

8

9

MANIFEST
3-6-9 contact method

1

2

3

1

2

3

4

5

6

1

2

3

4

5

6

7

8

9

Claim it!
TODAY'S DATE IS
_____

MANIFEST
3-6-9 contact method

1

2

3

1

2

3

4

5

6

1

2

3

4

5

6

7

8

9

MANIFEST
3-6-9 contact method

1

2

3

1

2

3

4

5

6

1

2

3

4

5

6

7

8

9

MANIFEST
3-6-9 contact method

1
2
3

1
2
3
4
5
6

1
2
3
4
5
6
7
8
9

MANIFEST

3-6-9 contact method

1

2

3

1

2

3

4

5

6

1

2

3

4

5

6

7

8

9

MANIFEST
3-6-9 contact method

1

2

3

1

2

3

4

5

6

1

2

3

4

5

6

7

8

9

MANIFEST
3-6-9 contact method

1

2

3

1

2

3

4

5

6

1

2

3

4

5

6

7

8

9

MANIFEST
3-6-9 contact method

1

2

3

1

2

3

4

5

6

1

2

3

4

5

6

7

8

9

MANIFEST
3-6-9 contact method

1

2

3

1

2

3

4

5

6

1

2

3

4

5

6

7

8

9

MANIFEST
3-6-9 contact method

1

2

3

1

2

3

4

5

6

1

2

3

4

5

6

7

8

9

MANIFEST
3-6-9 contact method

1
2
3

1
2
3
4
5
6

1
2
3
4
5
6
7
8
9

MANIFEST
3-6-9 contact method

1 _____

2 _____

3 _____

1 _____

2 _____

3 _____

4 _____

5 _____

6 _____

1 _____

2 _____

3 _____

4 _____

5 _____

6 _____

7 _____

8 _____

9 _____

MANIFEST

3-6-9 contact method

1

2

3

1

2

3

4

5

6

1

2

3

4

5

6

7

8

9

MANIFEST
3-6-9 contact method

1

2

3

1

2

3

4

5

6

1

2

3

4

5

6

7

8

9

MANIFEST
3-6-9 contact method

1

2

3

1

2

3

4

5

6

1

2

3

4

5

6

7

8

9

MANIFEST
3-6-9 contact method

1

2

3

1

2

3

4

5

6

1

2

3

4

5

6

7

8

9

MANIFEST
3-6-9 contact method

1

2

3

1

2

3

4

5

6

1

2

3

4

5

6

7

8

9

Claim it!
TODAY'S DATE IS

MANIFEST
3-6-9 contact method

1
2
3

1
2
3
4
5
6

1
2
3
4
5
6
7
8
9

MANIFEST
3-6-9 contact method

Claim it!
TODAY'S DATE IS

1

2

3

1

2

3

4

5

6

1

2

3

4

5

6

7

8

9

MANIFEST
3-6-9 contact method

1

2

3

1

2

3

4

5

6

1

2

3

4

5

6

7

8

9

MANIFEST

3-6-9 contact method

1

2

3

1

2

3

4

5

6

1

2

3

4

5

6

7

8

9

MANIFEST
3-6-9 contact method

1

2

3

1

2

3

4

5

6

1

2

3

4

5

6

7

8

9

MANIFEST
3-6-9 contact method

1
2
3

1
2
3
4
5
6

1
2
3
4
5
6
7
8
9

MANIFEST
3-6-9 contact method

1

2

3

1

2

3

4

5

6

1

2

3

4

5

6

7

8

9

MANIFEST

3-6-9 contact method

1

2

3

1

2

3

4

5

6

1

2

3

4

5

6

7

8

9

MANIFEST
3-6-9 contact method

1

2

3

1

2

3

4

5

6

1

2

3

4

5

6

7

8

9

MANIFEST

3-6-9 contact method

1

2

3

1

2

3

4

5

6

1

2

3

4

5

6

7

8

9

MANIFEST
3-6-9 contact method

1
2
3

1
2
3
4
5
6

1
2
3
4
5
6
7
8
9

MANIFEST

3-6-9 contact method

1
2
3

1
2
3
4
5
6

1
2
3
4
5
6
7
8
9

MANIFEST
3-6-9 contact method

1
2
3

1
2
3
4
5
6

1
2
3
4
5
6
7
8
9

MANIFEST

3-6-9 contact method

1

2

3

1

2

3

4

5

6

1

2

3

4

5

6

7

8

9

MANIFEST
3-6-9 contact method

1

2

3

1

2

3

4

5

6

1

2

3

4

5

6

7

8

9

MANIFEST
3-6-9 contact method

1

2

3

1

2

3

4

5

6

1

2

3

4

5

6

7

8

9

MANIFEST
3-6-9 contact method

1

2

3

1

2

3

4

5

6

1

2

3

4

5

6

7

8

9

MANIFEST

3-6-9 contact method

1
2
3

1
2
3
4
5
6

1
2
3
4
5
6
7
8
9

MANIFEST
3-6-9 contact method

1

2

3

1

2

3

4

5

6

1

2

3

4

5

6

7

8

9

MANIFEST
3-6-9 contact method

1

2

3

1

2

3

4

5

6

1

2

3

4

5

6

7

8

9

MANIFEST
3-6-9 contact method

1

2

3

1

2

3

4

5

6

1

2

3

4

5

6

7

8

9

MANIFEST
3-6-9 contact method

1

2

3

1

2

3

4

5

6

1

2

3

4

5

6

7

8

9

MANIFEST
3-6-9 contact method

1

2

3

1

2

3

4

5

6

1

2

3

4

5

6

7

8

9

MANIFEST
3-6-9 contact method

1

2

3

1

2

3

4

5

6

1

2

3

4

5

6

7

8

9

MANIFEST
3-6-9 contact method

1

2

3

1

2

3

4

5

6

1

2

3

4

5

6

7

8

9

MANIFEST
3-6-9 contact method

1

2

3

1

2

3

4

5

6

1

2

3

4

5

6

7

8

9

MANIFEST
3-6-9 contact method

1

2

3

1

2

3

4

5

6

1

2

3

4

5

6

7

8

9

MANIFEST
3-6-9 contact method

1

2

3

1

2

3

4

5

6

1

2

3

4

5

6

7

8

9

MANIFEST
3-6-9 contact method

1

2

3

1

2

3

4

5

6

1

2

3

4

5

6

7

8

9

MANIFEST
3-6-9 contact method

1

2

3

1

2

3

4

5

6

1

2

3

4

5

6

7

8

9

MANIFEST
3-6-9 contact method

1

2

3

1

2

3

4

5

6

1

2

3

4

5

6

7

8

9

MANIFEST
3-6-9 contact method

1

2

3

1

2

3

4

5

6

1

2

3

4

5

6

7

8

9

MANIFEST
3-6-9 contact method

1

2

3

1

2

3

4

5

6

1

2

3

4

5

6

7

8

9

MANIFEST
3-6-9 contact method

1

2

3

1

2

3

4

5

6

1

2

3

4

5

6

7

8

9

MANIFEST
3-6-9 contact method

1

2

3

1

2

3

4

5

6

1

2

3

4

5

6

7

8

9

MANIFEST
3-6-9 contact method

Claim it!
TODAY'S DATE IS
_____

1

2

3

1

2

3

4

5

6

1

2

3

4

5

6

7

8

9

MANIFEST
3-6-9 contact method

1

2

3

1

2

3

4

5

6

1

2

3

4

5

6

7

8

9

MANIFEST
3-6-9 contact method

1

2

3

1

2

3

4

5

6

1

2

3

4

5

6

7

8

9

MANIFEST
3-6-9 contact method

1

2

3

1

2

3

4

5

6

1

2

3

4

5

6

7

8

9

MANIFEST
3-6-9 contact method

1

2

3

1

2

3

4

5

6

1

2

3

4

5

6

7

8

9

MANIFEST
3-6-9 contact method

1

2

3

1

2

3

4

5

6

1

2

3

4

5

6

7

8

9

MANIFEST

3-6-9 contact method

1

2

3

1

2

3

4

5

6

1

2

3

4

5

6

7

8

9

MANIFEST
3-6-9 contact method

1

2

3

1

2

3

4

5

6

1

2

3

4

5

6

7

8

9

MANIFEST
3-6-9 contact method

1
2
3

1
2
3
4
5
6

1
2
3
4
5
6
7
8
9

MANIFEST
3-6-9 contact method

1

2

3

1

2

3

4

5

6

1

2

3

4

5

6

7

8

9

MANIFEST
3-6-9 contact method

1

2

3

1

2

3

4

5

6

1

2

3

4

5

6

7

8

9

MANIFEST
3-6-9 contact method

1
2
3

1
2
3
4
5
6

1
2
3
4
5
6
7
8
9

MANIFEST
3-6-9 contact method

1

2

3

1

2

3

4

5

6

1

2

3

4

5

6

7

8

9

MANIFEST
3-6-9 contact method

1
2
3

1
2
3
4
5
6

1
2
3
4
5
6
7
8
9

MANIFEST
3-6-9 contact method

1

2

3

1

2

3

4

5

6

1

2

3

4

5

6

7

8

9

MANIFEST
3-6-9 contact method

1

2

3

1

2

3

4

5

6

1

2

3

4

5

6

7

8

9

MANIFEST
3-6-9 contact method

Claim it!
TODAY'S DATE IS

1

2

3

1

2

3

4

5

6

1

2

3

4

5

6

7

8

9

MANIFEST
3-6-9 contact method

1

2

3

1

2

3

4

5

6

1

2

3

4

5

6

7

8

9

MANIFEST
3-6-9 contact method

Claim it!
TODAY'S DATE IS

1

2

3

1

2

3

4

5

6

1

2

3

4

5

6

7

8

9

MANIFEST
3-6-9 contact method

1

2

3

1

2

3

4

5

6

1

2

3

4

5

6

7

8

9

MANIFEST

3-6-9 contact method

1

2

3

1

2

3

4

5

6

1

2

3

4

5

6

7

8

9

MANIFEST
3-6-9 contact method

1

2

3

1

2

3

4

5

6

1

2

3

4

5

6

7

8

9

MANIFEST
3-6-9 contact method

1

2

3

1

2

3

4

5

6

1

2

3

4

5

6

7

8

9

MANIFEST
3-6-9 contact method

1

2

3

1

2

3

4

5

6

1

2

3

4

5

6

7

8

9

MANIFEST
3-6-9 contact method

1

2

3

1

2

3

4

5

6

1

2

3

4

5

6

7

8

9

MANIFEST
3-6-9 contact method

1

2

3

1

2

3

4

5

6

1

2

3

4

5

6

7

8

9

MANIFEST
3-6-9 contact method

Claim it!
TODAY'S DATE IS

1

2

3

1

2

3

4

5

6

1

2

3

4

5

6

7

8

9

MANIFEST
3-6-9 contact method

1

2

3

1

2

3

4

5

6

1

2

3

4

5

6

7

8

9

MANIFEST
3-6-9 contact method

1

2

3

1

2

3

4

5

6

1

2

3

4

5

6

7

8

9

MANIFEST
3-6-9 contact method

1

2

3

1

2

3

4

5

6

1

2

3

4

5

6

7

8

9

MANIFEST

3-6-9 contact method

Claim it!
TODAY'S DATE IS
_____

1

2

3

1

2

3

4

5

6

1

2

3

4

5

6

7

8

9

Made in the USA
Middletown, DE
15 May 2021